BENT'S FORT

MELVIN BACON AND DANIEL BLEGEN

BENT'S FORT

Crossroads of Cultures
on the Santa Fe Trail

Filter Press, LLC • Palmer Lake, Colorado

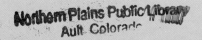

Filter Press, LLC
P.O. Box 95
Palmer Lake, CO 80133-0095
www.filterpressbooks.com

Cover: "Bent's Fort," oil painting by Jack Roberts, 1972. Photograph courtesy of The Denver Public Library, Western History Department.

Photographs courtesy of the Colorado Historical Society: pp. 11 (neg. no. F-24-374-BPF), 21 (top: neg. no. F-2 BPF, bottom: neg. no F-1535), 22 (neg. no. F-6537 BPF), 34 and 41 (from *Through the Country of the Comanche Indians*); Museum of New Mexico: p. 13 (neg. no. 87450); The Denver Public Library, Western History Department: pp. 14, 25; North Wind Picture Archives: pp. 19, 33, 50, 56; Western History Collections, University of Oklahoma Library: p. 23; authors' collection: p. 29; Missouri Historical Society, St. Louis: pp. 39 (*Buffalo Hunt* by Carl Wimar, 1861. acc. no. 1950.116.2.2), 46 (acc. no. 1933.1.1); Special Collections Division, The University of Texas at Arlington Libraries, Arlington, Texas: p. 48; State Historical Society of Missouri, Columbia: p. 53; Melvin L. Bacon: p. 62 (top); Daniel Blegen: p. 62 (bottom); diagram on pp. 64-65 adapted from :"Bent's Old Fort" published by the National Park Service, U.S. Department of the Interior. Map by Joe LeMonnier.

Publisher's Cataloging-in-Publication
(Provided by Quality Books, Inc.)

Bacon, Melvin.
    Bent's Fort : crossroads of cultures on the Santa Fe
trail / Melvin Bacon and Daniel Blegen.
    p. cm.
    Includes bibliographical references and index.
    SUMMARY: Drawing on journals of the 1840s, the
authors describe the life of an important trading center
on the Santa Fe Trail, where U.S., Mexican, and Indian
cultures mingled at a key time in American history,
    LCCN 2001099397
    ISBN 0-86541-062-3

    1. Bent's Fort (Colo.)—Juvenile literature.
2. Santa Fe National Historic Trail--Juvenile literature.
[1. Bent's Fort (Colo.) 2. Frontier and pioneer life.
3. Santa Fe National Historic Trail.]   I. Blegen,
Daniel. II. Title.

F782.A7B33 2002   978.8'95
                        QBI33-275

To Vicki, my first reader and best critic,
and to Tania, Erin, and Kelly.
D.B.

To Debi, Sarah, and Joseph, and to
Robert L. Brown, who first sparked
my interest in the American West.
M.B.

Acknowledgments

The notion of writing this book began during a twenty-four-hour "rendezvous" at Bent's Fort in the summer of 1993. Chief Ranger Alejandra Aldred of Bent's Old Fort National Historic Site provided us with a valuable re-creation of life there in 1846. Many thanks go to her for that learning experience. We must also thank the Social Studies Education Consortium of Boulder, Colorado, for including us in The American West Institute, funded by the National Endowment for the Humanities. Special thanks to those at SSEC—James Giese, Barbara Miller, Lori Eastman, and Betsy Glade. Thanks for insights and inspiration go to Gary Holthaus, Patricia Limerick, and Elliott West. Finally, thanks to those who helped proofread the manuscript, especially Cathy Cloepfil.

Melvin Bacon and
Daniel Blegen

Contents

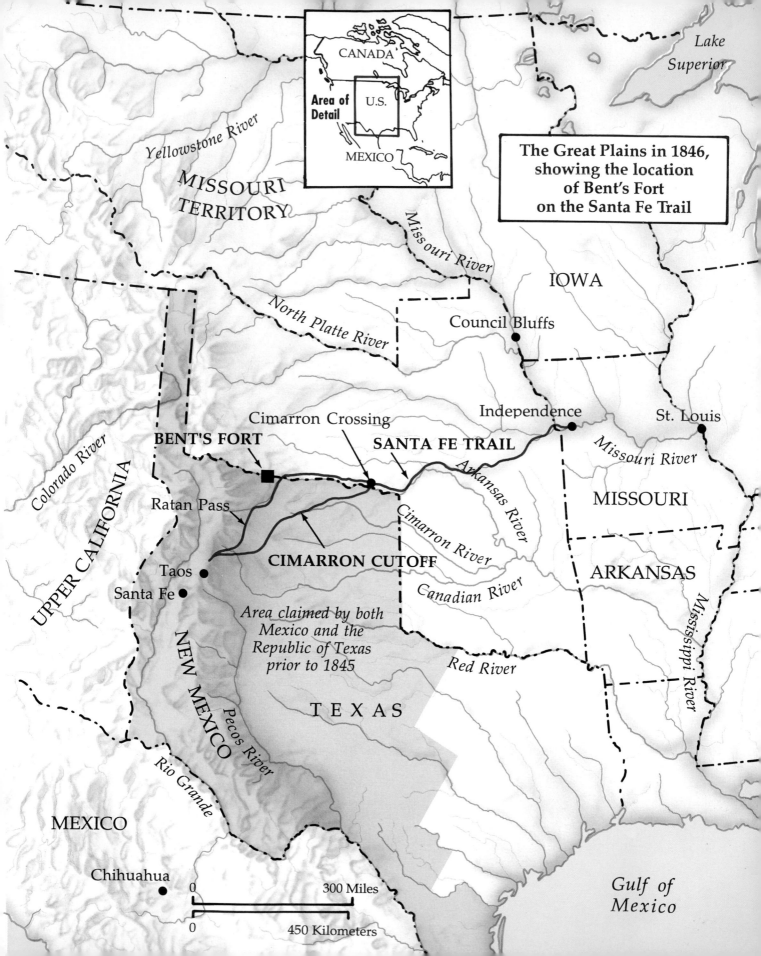

Yellowstone River

MISSOURI TERRITORY

Missouri River

CANADA

Area of Detail

U.S.

MEXICO

Lake Superior

The Great Plains in 1846, showing the location of Bent's Fort on the Santa Fe Trail

North Platte River

IOWA

Council Bluffs

Colorado River

Cimarron Crossing

BENT'S FORT

SANTA FE TRAIL

Independence

St. Louis

Missouri River

Arkansas River

MISSOURI

Ratan Pass

Cimarron River

CIMARRON CUTOFF

UPPER CALIFORNIA

Taos

Santa Fe

Canadian River

ARKANSAS

Mississippi River

Area claimed by both Mexico and the Republic of Texas prior to 1845

NEW MEXICO

Pecos River

Red River

T E X A S

Rio Grande

MEXICO

Chihuahua

0   300 Miles

0   450 Kilometers

Gulf of Mexico

1 A Woman at the Crossroads of Cultures

The year 1846 was an exciting one for eighteen-year-old Susan Shelby Magoffin. It was the year Susan would accompany her husband, Samuel, on a trading expedition to Mexico. It was also the year that Susan and Samuel Magoffin were expecting the arrival of their first baby.

The only overland route to Mexico was a bumpy dirt path called the Santa Fe Trail. It began at Independence, Missouri, and stretched south and west across the prairies to the Mexican town of Santa Fe. One of the few settlements along the trail was a trading post called Bent's Fort. The fort sat along the north bank of the Arkansas River in what is now the southeast corner of the state of Colorado. Until the United States went to war against Mexico, the Arkansas River formed part of the boundary between the two countries. Bent's Fort was an important stop on the Santa Fe Trail. Just a short distance beyond the fort the trail curved to the south, crossed the river, and entered Mexico. Little did Susan

Magoffin suspect when she left Independence that her travels would be interrupted for twelve full days at Bent's Fort during the eventful summer of 1846.

The 800-mile (1,280-kilometer) Santa Fe Trail had been open since 1821, but few women from the United States had traveled it when Susan Magoffin accompanied her husband to Mexico. She wrote about the trip each day in a diary kept along the trail. "My journal tells a story tonight different from what it has ever done before," Susan wrote on an evening in June before her departure. "From the city of New York to the plains of Mexico, is a stride that I myself can scarcely realize." Her diary has preserved for us a record of daily events along the Santa Fe Trail, including buffalo hunts through prairie grasses "so tall in some places as to conceal a man's waist." Susan's diary also gives us some of the best descriptions of Bent's Fort and the people of many cultures who met there.

As Susan wrote in her diary after a few days on the trail, ". . . now for a bit of my wonderful travels so far."

Susan Magoffin's journey on the Santa Fe Trail was anything but lonely. "We now numbered . . . quite a force," she wrote a few days out from the trailhead. Indeed, their trade goods filled fourteen wagons, each pulled by six yokes (pairs) of oxen. It took twenty men to drive the wagons and to manage the two horses, nine mules, and two hundred oxen. The Magoffins' personal belongings filled an additional wagon, and a covered carriage known as a dearborn carried their maid, Jane. Also traveling with Susan was her dog, named Ring. Susan described Ring as white with brown spots and of "noble descent." He proved to be a good watchdog along the trail.

Because Samuel Magoffin's business was successful, he and Susan were able to travel the prairies in some comfort. Susan

Susan Magoffin was the first white woman to travel the Santa Fe Trail.
Her diary describing life at Bent's Fort was preserved by one of her daughters
and published eighty years after she wrote it.

rode in a private carriage. When the caravan stopped to make camp, three Mexican servants set up a tent for her and Samuel. Susan slept in her own bed, which she had brought from the East. The bed was unloaded from a wagon each evening and reloaded each morning. "It is the life of a wandering princess, mine," she boasted in her diary.

However, this privileged journey was not without irritations for her. "Snakes and mosquitoes," she admitted, "are the only disagreeable parts of my prairie life." And at night Susan was glad to have Ring by her bed when wolves prowled close to camp. Her days on the trail echoed with "the cracking of whips, lowing of cattle, braying of mules," and the "whooping and hallowing of men." Most days blistered with heat. Driving rains on other days turned the trail to mud and forced the wagons to stop altogether. But, she wrote, "As bad as it all is, I enjoy it still. I look upon it as one of the varieties of life, and as that is always spice, of course, it must be enjoyed."

Along the Santa Fe Trail the Magoffins sometimes shared the pathway with other traders' wagons heading the other way. By chance, on the twelfth day of the trip, they met Charles Bent, who was riding east along the trail. He and his brother William and their friend Ceran St. Vrain operated Bent, St. Vrain, and Company and the Bent's Fort trading post. Charles was returning to Independence on company business. Susan took advantage of the chance meeting to ask Charles Bent to deliver a quickly written letter to her father "back in the states."

The Santa Fe Trail was busier than usual during the summer of 1846. There were 130 merchant wagons moving toward Santa Fe. All the traders on the trail that summer traveled with the knowledge that in May the United States had officially declared war against Mexico. In addition to the hardships of the trail, traders had to deal with the fear of becoming entangled in fighting

This etching depicts a convoy of covered wagons under way on the Santa Fe Trail during the 1830s. In the years following its opening in 1821, the trail was sparsely traveled, but by the late 1860s as many as five thousand wagons a year passed along the rigorous route.

between the armies of the two countries. The Magoffins at one point shared the trail with two companies of American soldiers working their way to Santa Fe.

It took the Magoffins forty-five difficult days on the trail to reach Bent's Fort. It is no wonder that on July 27, Susan was relieved to see its solid adobe walls rising above the banks of the Arkansas River. "Well it fills my idea of an ancient castle," she told her diary. And although Bent's Fort was really just a trading post, it did resemble the castle of an ancient king.

After forty-five days on the trail, it is no wonder that Susan Magoffin found the sight of Bent's Fort like her "idea of an ancient castle." The round corner towers (called bastions) as well as the watchtower topped by a bell tower and an American flag over the front gate did indeed give an impression of grandeur as it loomed into sight from the wilderness.

On July 27, 1846, a massive wooden gate in the east wall of the fort creaked on its hinges. Through the open gate and into the fort's central plaza walked Susan and Samuel Magoffin. Bent's Fort was teeming with people. "The shoeing of horses, the neighing and braying of mules, the crying of children, [and] the scolding and fighting of men," Susan complained, "are all enough to turn my head." Craftsmen worked noisily. Mexican women tended open fires from which came inviting aromas and the promise of a hot meal. All talked excitedly, greeting the fort's latest guests and asking for news from the East.

The fort provided sleeping quarters and hot meals for traders who might have camped out for months before reaching it. At Bent's Fort, craftsmen repaired wagons and travelers bought supplies. White trappers sold beaver pelts brought down from the Rocky Mountains. Mexican traders offered exotic goods from distant lands, and Native American hunters presented buffalo robes by the hundreds. All hoped for fair deals from the trading company of Bent and St. Vrain.

In addition, the fort had been contracted by the United States Army to house soldiers who had become ill marching or riding along the trail. These soldiers belonged to a part of the U.S. Army called the Army of the West. The recovering soldiers rested in their second-floor quarters or drilled halfheartedly in the dusty plaza.

Charles and William Bent and Ceran St. Vrain had been operating their business at the Bent's Fort location for fourteen years by the summer of Susan Magoffin's visit. The bulk of their early trading had been with white trappers, often called mountain men. By 1846, however, considerably more of the trade was with Native American tribes such as the Arapahos and the Cheyennes.

On July 30, 1846, Susan Magoffin passed her nineteenth birthday at Bent's Fort. But it was not to be a happy day. She told her diary, "I am sick!" "Strange sensations" in her head, back, and hips forced her to bed for the day. The Bents provided Susan and her husband with a large corner room on the second floor of the fort. Her own bed and other pieces of furniture were brought from the Magoffins' wagons to make her more comfortable. But even medicines given by a doctor at the fort failed to ease Susan's severe pains. It became obvious that the pains meant Susan would lose the baby she was expecting, and the child was born dead about midnight.

Susan, of course, was saddened by the loss of her baby. However, a few days later she was writing in her diary again, thinking of others at the fort and commenting on events. Susan wrote with great admiration about another woman at Bent's Fort, who gave birth to a healthy baby on the same day that she lost hers. "My situation was very different from that of an Indian woman in the room below me," she wrote. "She gave birth to a fine healthy baby . . . and in half an hour after she went to the River and bathed herself and it, and this she has continued each day since. It is truly astonishing what customs will do."

2 Mountain Men and Beaver Hats

Long before the building of their fort, the brothers William and Charles Bent had come west to trap beavers for pelts. From the early 1800s on, firms such as the Missouri Fur Company, founded by Manuel Lisa, and the American Fur Company, founded by John Jacob Astor, sent trappers up the Mississippi and Missouri river valleys. The companies competed fiercely and often dishonestly. It is said that President Zachary Taylor called the American Fur Company's bosses "the greatest scoundrels the world ever knew."

The fur trade had flourished years before Astor's company was formed. In 1754 the French and Indian War had erupted over trapping rights in the Ohio River valley. Then, in 1776, British authorities had angered colonial trappers by closing areas west of the Appalachian Mountains.

The animal most often trapped for its fur was the beaver. By the early 1800s, Europeans and Americans were demanding that almost all fashionable clothes include fur. Fur decorated everything from the collars of men's coats to the hems of ladies' dresses. However, the popularity of men's felt hats produced the largest market for beaver pelts (the felt was made from beaver fur). Because of the great demand, trappers sometimes killed all the beavers in one area of a river. Then they were forced to set traps farther upstream and eventually as far west as the Rocky Mountains.

Trapping was difficult work. Most trapping was done during the winter, when the beaver pelts were thickest. The mountain men had to set traps in icy mountain streams. They had to skin and stretch and dress (tan) the pelts and bind them for shipment. The trappers themselves had to transport the pelts hundreds of miles to St. Louis or to the town of Taos in Mexico to sell them. Although they could sell other animal hides, beaver was the most profitable. Beaver pelts often sold at from six to eight dollars each. Buffalo hides, although much larger, brought only three or four dollars each.

The trappers faced personal hardships too: loneliness, disease, starvation, attacks by Indian raiders, and the harsh weather of the winter trapping season. Most men trapped for only a few years. Some made enough money to establish themselves in more traditional businesses back East. Others did not survive long enough to enjoy any profit.

Trappers began to see that an easier way of obtaining hides and pelts would be to trade with Indian hunters. In addition to their usual gear, trappers began carrying trade items such as flour, cloth, tobacco, and trinkets. Trappers would trade these items for hides and pelts acquired by the Indians. White trappers also began to trade whiskey and guns. The Indians were interested in both, but both contributed to problems between people, as they still can today.

A trader's camp showing the tents and wagons of the traders nestled among the teepees of the Native Americans.

Of course, trading did bring together many different people as friends. William Ashley, a competitor of John Jacob Astor's, started a yearly gathering of trappers, traders, and Native Americans from all over the West. Agents from various fur companies also attended, arriving with wagons full of trade goods. Ashley's gathering was called a rendezvous.

The rendezvous proved beneficial for all concerned. It enabled trappers to make fewer selling trips. It gave the trappers and Native Americans alike a chance to meet more trading partners. Fur companies could transport hides and pelts from a yearly rendezvous to eastern markets in fewer, larger shipments.

The rendezvous offered more than just a time for trading. Games of skill were held, and there was much gambling, whiskey drinking, and wild behavior. For ten days to two weeks the rendezvous party continued. Finally, a location was chosen for the next year's meeting, and everyone went his own way.

Then, in the early 1830s, fashions changed. Suddenly men's hats were no longer being made from beaver pelts, but from silk. The demand for beaver went down rapidly, and the price for a pelt dropped from six dollars to about one.

Mountain men stopped dealing in beaver pelts and began trading with the Native American tribes for buffalo robes. Buffalo robes were furry buffalo hides from which the flesh had been cleaned. People in the East bought buffalo robes to use as rugs in their homes and as lap robes to keep their legs warm in winter weather when riding in sleighs and wagons.

William Bent preferred this new "Indian trade" to the beaver trapping he had done earlier. Sometime between 1828 and 1830 he built a wooden stockade near the present city of Pueblo, Colorado. Made of tall cedar posts driven into the ground, the stockade enclosed three houses. William stored goods there and waited for Indian traders to arrive. Business was not good. Too late William realized that the stockade sat in an area that was a kind of "no man's land" between the Cheyennes and Arapahos and their enemies the Utes. Few members of these tribes ever even came close to the stockade.

Meanwhile, Charles Bent had mastered the business of trading between St. Louis and Santa Fe. In 1831, for example, he made five trips along the Santa Fe Trail. To begin a trip in St. Louis or Independence, traders like Charles often had to borrow money to buy trade items. Along the trail were hostile raiding parties, little water, and occasional bad weather. When they entered Santa Fe,

William Bent's somewhat ferocious look belies a man who cared a great deal about the Native American traders with whom he dealt. In his later years, he was made an Indian agent for the government and worked tirelessly to defend the people whose world had been all but crushed by the advance of white settlement.

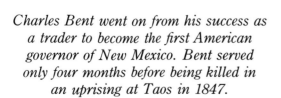

Charles Bent went on from his success as a trader to become the first American governor of New Mexico. Bent served only four months before being killed in an uprising at Taos in 1847.

Ceran St. Vrain, the third partner in Bent, St. Vrain, and Company, turned his share of the business over to William Bent in the late 1840s after a falling out involving St. Vrain's desire to sell the fort to the U.S. government.

they had to pay a business tax to the Mexican government. Then, after making it back, traders had to sell the hides and pelts quickly to repay the money they had borrowed in the first place. If they returned at a time when prices were low, they made little if any profit.

Charles Bent worked out solutions to these problems. In 1830 he proposed to his friend Ceran St. Vrain that they form a partnership. Later the partnership would be called Bent, St. Vrain, and Company. St. Vrain would remain in Santa Fe to do the actual trading, and Charles Bent would supervise the wagons on the trail. A permanent fort, like the stockade built by his brother William, seemed a good idea to Charles.

William and Charles Bent, accompanied by their younger brothers George and Robert, discussed building a more permanent structure on the site of the stockade. While they were talking about the possibilities for the business, a group of Cheyenne warriors of the Hairy Rope Clan paid the Bents a visit. At previous meetings a Cheyenne named Yellow Wolf had taken a special liking to the brothers. He had come to like them so much that he now gave each of the Bents an Indian name, a Cheyenne practice that indicated great honor. He gave the name Green Bird to the younger brother, Robert. George would be Little Beaver. Charles was called White Hat, possibly because Yellow Wolf saw him as a leader. The Kiowas had already given William the name

This sketch of Yellow Wolf, the Cheyenne warrior who first suggested the location for Bent's trading fort, was made in 1845 by U.S. Army lieutenant James W. Abert.

Bent Hook Nose, but the Cheyenne Yellow Wolf labeled him Little White Man because of his small size.

Yellow Wolf was himself a successful horse thief and trader. He became excited about the idea of a permanent trading fort, but he felt that the location of the stockade was not as promising as a site called Big Timbers. Big Timbers was about 90 miles (145 kilometers) east of the stockade, on the Arkansas River. Huge cottonwood trees there could supply wood for shelter and fuel, and there was much grass for livestock. Furthermore, the buffalo were plentiful at Big Timbers. The Cheyenne men hunted at Big Timbers, and the women could prepare buffalo hides for trading. Charles Bent knew that other tribes also passed through the area.

The Bent brothers, however, did not take Yellow Wolf's suggestion. They chose a different location on the Arkansas River. Their choice was on the Santa Fe Trail and right across the river from Mexico. Pelts and other goods from Santa Fe could be stored safely in a fort at this location until prices were high in the East and goods could be sold there at a profit. Trading could still be conducted at their location with the Cheyennes as well as with the Arapahos, Prairie Apaches, Utes, Comanches, and Kiowas. Although business proved good at the Bents' chosen site, William later regretted not locating the trading fort at Big Timbers, as his friend Yellow Wolf had suggested.

Completed during 1833 and 1834, Bent's Fort became the largest structure of its time between Missouri and the Pacific Ocean. It was built of adobe bricks, made with a mixture of mud, straw, wool, and water and formed in wooden molds and dried in the sun. Mexican workers from Taos made the bricks on the spot and erected the massive fort. These workers were paid no more than five or ten dollars a month for the difficult job, and most of their pay was in the form of trade goods such as calico cloth, gunpowder, lead shot, and coffee.

The walls of the fort were built 15 feet (about 4.5 meters) high and almost 3 feet (1 meter) thick. The outside of the fort measured about 137 feet by 178 feet (42 by 54 meters). An opening in the front wall was protected by a wooden gate 9 feet (almost 3 meters) wide and 7 feet (2 meters) high. Over the front gate were a watchtower, an American flag, and a dinner bell. At two corners of the fort stood large round towers called bastions. Each bastion was equipped with a small cannon to protect the fort from potential invaders. A livestock corral was given a more natural defense—some very prickly cactus planted along the top of its walls.

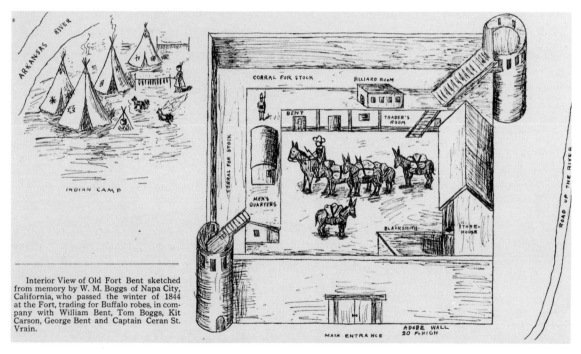

Interior View of Old Fort Bent sketched from memory by W. M. Boggs of Napa City, California, who passed the winter of 1844 at the Fort, trading for Buffalo robes, in company with William Bent, Tom Boggs, Kit Carson, George Bent and Captain Ceran St. Vrain.

An interior view of Bent's Fort sketched from memory by W. M. Boggs of Napa City, California. Boggs spent the winter of 1844 at the fort, trading for buffalo robes, with the Bents and St. Vrain as well as Kit Carson.

The front gate opened into a central *placita* (open plaza) surrounded by living rooms; a kitchen and dining room; carpentry, blacksmith, and tailor shops; storage rooms; and the all-important trade room. Susan Magoffin described this room, which she called a parlor, in her diary:

> There are no chairs but a cushion next to the wall on two sides, so the company all set around in a circle. There is no other furniture than a table on which stands a bucket of water free to all. Any water that may be left in the cup after drinking is unceremoniously tossed onto the floor.

A second floor of apartments was built along one wall of the *placita*. A privileged few were admitted to a second-floor bar, where the men could play billiards. There was even an adobe icehouse, built along the river to keep meat cool and provide the luxury of iced drinks in summer, when temperatures often soared to over 100°F (nearly 40°C).

In the fall of 1833 the construction of Bent's Fort was almost finished. On the night of November 12, as if the stars themselves were announcing the completion of the fort, hundreds of silent arrows of light flamed above the prairie and walls of Bent's Fort. Those at the fort must have watched in wonder as one of the biggest meteor showers on record lit the sky. Though they may not have known it that night, the stargazers at Bent's Fort were seeing the same heavenly display as watchers at both ends of the Santa Fe Trail and across North America. And just as the Santa Fe Trail connected many different cultures, so the meteor shower of 1833 connected its many watchers.

The meteor shower seemed to carry a mysterious message that the people of each culture read differently. At the eastern starting point of the trail, in Independence, Missouri, white settlers had been mistreating members of the Mormon Church.

These Missouri citizens read the meteor shower as heaven's disapproval of their actions. At the western end of the trail, in Santa Fe, Mexican citizens believed the meteor shower announced a curse upon them because their government had denied certain rights to the Catholic Church.

In the middle of the Santa Fe Trail, at Bent's Fort, a group of Cheyennes was camped outside the new adobe walls. They also read the meteor shower as a sign in the sky. In a recent battle against some Pawnees, these Cheyennes had lost four sacred arrows that they believed had protected them from harm. The falling stars, they thought, must be a sign that they were now totally defenseless against their enemies. The Cheyenne women and children cried in fear. The young men dressed for battle, sure that they would die bravely before the night was over.

Traders in competition with Bent, St. Vrain, and Company needed no heavenly signs to see the importance of Bent's "adobe castle." William Laidlaw, at the American Fur Company's Fort Pierre in what is now South Dakota, recognized the competition that Bent's Fort would introduce to the trading business. A few months after the meteor shower, in January 1834, Laidlaw wrote to fellow trader Pierre Chouteau: "I understand from the Sioux that Charles Bent has built a fort upon the Arkanzas [sic] . . . and if judiciously carried on it cannot fail to be very injurious to the trade in this part of the country." Like an explosion of meteors on an autumn night, Bent's Fort would light the vast prairie, changing it forever.

3 Work and Play at Bent's Fort

The fort was officially called Fort William by the operators of Bent, St. Vrain, and Company. This name was in honor of William Bent, who was largely responsible for trading there. It was called simply Bent's Fort by everyone else. To make the business as profitable as possible, William had to make all visitors to the fort feel welcome and comfortable. Between 1834 and 1849 all kinds of people gathered there. In fact, seven different languages were spoken at Bent's Fort: Cheyenne, Comanche, English, French, Sioux, Spanish, and Ute. Most visitors came to trade. Some used the fort as a kind of hotel, the only one on the vast plains. In the summer of 1846 the Army of the West used Bent's Fort as a hospital for its sick soldiers, as a supply depot, and as a jumping-off place for the invasion of Mexico.

Race, religion, and color had less to do with a person's social rank at Bent's Fort than in other places. For example, even though Andrew and Dick Green had been brought west as slaves

William Bent with Arapaho chief Little Raven and the chief's three children. Bent was an Indian agent in the years after the destruction of the Old Fort.

by Charles Bent, they were accepted at the fort for their accomplishments. Like Jim Beckwourth, an African-American mountain man, they did not find the color of their skin held against them. Charlotte Green, Dick's wife and the fort's cook, became well-known across the prairies for her dancing skills, as well as for the delicious meals she served. Charlotte called herself the "only lady in de whole damn Indian country."

Of course, there was a social ranking at the fort. Although people of many nationalities, races, and customs worked within the walls of Bent's Fort, they did not always mix. At the top of the fort's social structure were the owners and their families. Younger brothers, such as George and Robert Bent and Marcellin St. Vrain, were brought up to become trusted company assistants. Those who married into the families were also included in the business. Independent visiting trappers were treated as equals and rounded out the fort's uppermost social level.

The next social group at the fort was made up of hunters, trail guides, hired trappers, traders, and tradesmen. These people were considered employees of the company.

Mexican laborers tended livestock. Mexican women repaired the fort's adobe walls. Some people were hired to gather cottonwood logs from along the river or to collect buffalo "chips" from the prairie to provide fuel for the cooking and heating fires that burned throughout the fort. These part-time employees had no real social standing at the fort.

The number of people living at the fort varied. There were often fewer than twenty people there. Some residents traveled the Santa Fe Trail, visited Native American encampments, or roamed the mountains. When most of the fort's residents were at "home," the population rose to about two hundred.

It was common for Bent's Fort to offer its hospitality to travelers such as Susan and Samuel Magoffin. Because Samuel was an independent trader and because his wife had become ill, Susan was given a guest room. In her diary, Susan noted: "It is quite roomy. Like the others it has a dirt floor." In addition to guest rooms, there were well-appointed private quarters for the owners and their families. Rooms were provided for the families of married employees. Single men were housed together in dormitories that slept six to eight.

Others who were just passing along the Santa Fe Trail, such as freighters, were not assigned sleeping rooms. Although these people could bring their wagons and their livestock into the *placita* at night for safety, Bent's Fort was for them simply one more trail campsite.

Native Americans were essential to the fort's trading. Still, except for the Indian wives and children of some of the white men living in the fort, no Indians were allowed to stay within its walls overnight, for reasons of security.

The dining room illustrated the fort's social rankings. The owners and their families, the independent traders, and special guests ate first. Once they had finished, hunters and trappers and tradesmen were served. Those who were not part of these groups were not invited to the dining room. They had to prepare their own food and eat it in their living quarters.

Bent, St. Vrain, and Company employed a full-time staff of mechanics and craftsmen. A carpenter, a blacksmith, a gunsmith, a wheelwright, and a tailor could usually be found at work in the fort. Black Charlotte, as Charlotte Green was called throughout the Southwest, was another full-time staff member. Occasionally a barber cut hair and shaved whiskers at the fort. Living quarters were provided for these workers and their families.

Others came to work at the fort on a temporary basis. They included herders, hunters, and bullwhackers (men who drove teams of oxen).

There was a well within the fort walls. Susan Magoffin described its "fine water . . . especially with ice." Water was also brought daily from the river, a job done by an old Irishman whose toes had been frozen off. After bringing water from the river, he spent the rest of his day hauling trash to a spot outside the walls.

Bent, St. Vrain, and Company bought and sold horses. Some were bought from travelers. Most were acquired from Indians who had stolen them. Among Plains Indians, horse stealing was an honorable activity, and in many tribes a man's wealth was judged by the number of horses he called his own. At the fort, livestock were kept in the adobe corral at night and then driven great distances along the river to feed during the day.

In addition to horses, the fort kept oxen, milk cows, chickens, turkeys, pigeons, and sometimes Mexican goats and sheep. These animals produced mountains of manure that had to be hauled away—for obvious reasons of sanitation and because as manure dries it becomes a fire hazard. George Bent once brought peacocks to the fort. The local Indians were fascinated and shocked by the birds' bright feathers and shrill calls.

Several times there were attempts to grow a vegetable garden just outside the fort's walls. These efforts failed when loose livestock trampled or ate the crops and local Indians helped themselves. Dried beans were the main vegetable prepared by Black Charlotte. Sometimes Mexican traders brought other dried vegetables or fruits, such as raisins. However, the diet of those at the fort consisted mainly of meat.

At the fort's store two kinds of trade were conducted. The first was the Indian trade. The Indians could obtain goods such as knives, blankets, axes, powder horns, guns, kettles, and beads in exchange for their beaver pelts and buffalo robes. The second type, the Santa Fe trade, included selling to Mexican and white traders imported rum or the stills to make alcohol. It also involved the sale of cloth, clothing, sugar, coffee, tea, rice, cutlery, and kitchen utensils. These goods could be bought with Mexican gold or silver at the fort. The company also transported these goods to Santa Fe to sell them there.

During her stay, Susan Magoffin observed other people's customs, some of which she found disturbing. On her first evening at the fort she visited a group of women, including the wife of George Bent. Susan was amazed when one of the women combed her hair in the presence of a man. She was shocked when the woman then applied "oil or grease of some kind" to her head. Susan added, "It is not exaggeration to say it almost *driped* [sic] from her hair to the floor." Susan Magoffin also found other activities at the fort in conflict with her personal values. She expressed dismay at the gambling she suspected took place in the fort's billiard room and out at its horse racetrack.

Native Americans brought buffalo skins and beaver pelts to the fort's store to exchange mainly for goods such as guns or kettles that were made by the white community.

Cheyenne women perform a scalp dance at Bent's Fort, presumably for the entertainment of the guests. The drawing was done at the fort in 1846 by Lieutenant James W. Abert.

Gambling was just one form of entertainment created by the residents. Storytelling, or "yarn spinning," was popular. The more outrageous the story, the better. Playing tricks on others was still another form of amusement. One Bent's Fort resident, Old Belzy Dodd, who wore a wig on his bald head, enjoyed staring at Indian visitors until he got their attention. Then he would whip off his wig and yell, "White-man-who-scalps-himself!"

Dances, held almost nightly, were one activity that brought all the fort's social classes together. Visitor Lewis Garrard wrote that Black Charlotte and Rosalie, the carpenter's "half-breed" wife, were "swung rudely and gently in the mazes of the contra dance."

Despite differences among the fort's residents, it was a place where all could work, struggle, fight, and play. Perhaps Susan Magoffin said it best: "The Fort is not such a bad place after all. There are some good people in and about it."

4 Native Americans of the Plains

The woman whose baby was born at Bent's Fort during Susan Magoffin's stay there was probably a member of the Southern Cheyenne tribe. It was the custom of the Cheyennes to bathe daily in a river or stream, even when that meant breaking through a layer of ice in cold winter weather. Susan Magoffin's astonishment at this woman is just one indication of the differences between white travelers on the Santa Fe Trail and the people of other cultures they encountered.

Customs and beliefs also differed greatly from one Native American tribe to the next. Different tribes spoke different languages, and within tribes there were often many different dialects, or ways of speaking. The Sioux and the Cheyennes, for example, could not understand each other's language. The Sioux called the Cheyennes the *Sha-hi-e-na,* meaning "people speaking language not understood." The Sioux word *Sha-hi-e-na* is the origin of the English word *"Cheyenne."* When the Cheyennes spoke about themselves, they used their own word, *T-sis-tsis-tas,* which simply means "the people."

Each tribe in the West had its own values and its own spiritual beliefs. Some tribes lived comfortably, while others struggled for survival. Some became fierce warriors, while others were inclined to be peaceful. In the early 1800s the Cheyennes called the Arapahos the Cloud People because they were so peaceful and generous. The Cheyennes themselves, by the 1840s, were known as savage warriors who often fought with other tribes, such as the Kiowas and the Pawnees, just for the deadly excitement of battle. The Arapahos, Kiowas, Pawnees, and other tribes all visited Bent's Fort, but surprisingly it was the fighting Cheyennes who became most welcome there.

The history of the Cheyenne people, like that of all the Plains tribes, is a long one. As early as the 1600s the Cheyennes lived in what is now Minnesota. They had no guns. They had no horses. These Cheyenne ancestors were pushed from their forest homeland by white settlers and then pushed farther and farther west by the Sioux, Cree, and Assiniboin tribes.

According to native tradition, the Assiniboins were the first people to attack the Cheyennes with rifles, and encountering guns caused the peaceful Cheyennes to change. Suddenly they said, "Now we have fought with these people. They attacked us and have killed some of us. After this let us fight with all people we meet, and we shall become great men."

Near the Black Hills of present-day South Dakota, the Cheyennes first acquired horses. Horses caused the second major change in the Cheyenne way of life, enabling the people to move farther and faster over the plains. With both guns and horses, the Cheyenne men were the feared warriors they had vowed to become.

Horses also made the Cheyenne men more successful in hunting the buffalo. Better hunting, in turn, led to many other changes. For example, buffalo meat became their main source of food. The Cheyenne women learned how to prepare buffalo hides by tanning, a process of cleaning them for practical uses. A number of tanned hides could be sewed together and then stretched around a frame of wooden poles to form a movable home called a tepee. For the Plains tribes the tepee was an important invention. *Tepee* comes from a Sioux word meaning the "place where a person lives." Well-made tepees were cool in summer and warm in winter. Horses could easily carry the tepee hides and poles. This enabled the Cheyennes to follow the wandering buffalo herds on which they had grown to depend.

The Cheyenne people had once planted crops and lived in one location. Because of the horse and the buffalo, the Cheyennes became nomads—people who move often, never building permanent homes in any one spot.

It was the trade in buffalo robes that brought white businessmen like William Bent to the Cheyennes. Bent and others often traveled hundreds of miles on horseback to reach their villages. William Bent especially liked trading with the Cheyennes. He traded manufactured goods from cities back east in return for their buffalo robes. Since the Cheyenne hunters did most of their hunting in winter, when the buffalo grew their heaviest coats, winter was also the busy season for traders like William Bent.

Daily life in a Cheyenne village was in some ways similar to life at Bent's Fort. Every member of the tribe had his or her own job to do. The men did the hunting and protected the village from attack. The women prepared the important buffalo hides and robes. They gathered the firewood for cooking and warmth. In winter the women gathered tree bark for the horses to eat when no grass was available. It was the Cheyenne women who built and

Traders' insatiable hunger for more and more buffalo robes led the Cheyenne to overhunt. Professional white hunters compounded the problem. Between 1850 to 1890 the buffalo population dropped from 20 million to just over 500.

took care of the tepees, did the cooking, sewed clothes, and cared for the children.

The boys would be put in charge of the horses grazing near the village, and the girls would help their mothers with chores. But mostly the children were allowed to play. Girls would play with dolls made of stuffed deerskin. The boys would play "war," riding stick "horses." They would wrestle or play a kicking game in which the object was to jump into the air and kick an opponent. Throwing games were popular, too. One such game involved darts, which were thrown at a target placed about 50 yards (40 to 50 meters) away. During the winter trading season all the Cheyenne children would coast down snow-covered hills on sleds made from buffalo ribs or wood or pieces of rawhide.

The arrival of white traders in a camp would disrupt the normal village activities. Curious children would gather around the traders, and the barking of the tribe's dogs would alert everyone in the village to their presence.

On one such day in the winter of 1845–46, William Bent entered a particular Cheyenne village many days' ride from Bent's Fort. William Bent, like the Cheyennes themselves, disliked staying in one spot for too long. Even during the coldest weather he left the comforts of his fort to find villages where he could trade.

Before leaving the fort he packed trade goods on a number of slow but steady mules. After each day's ride William and his partners made camp and slept between furry buffalo robes on the frozen prairie ground. Campfires were kept burning all night but gave little warmth, and in the darkness beyond the circle of campfire light, wolves prowled and howled.

William Bent was especially welcomed at this Cheyenne village. Nine years earlier he had married a young woman from the village. Her name was *Mis-stan-stur*.

The Cheyenne woman Mis-stan-stur *was the wife of William Bent.*
In English her name meant Owl Woman.
She was the daughter of Gray Thunder, the group's medicine man.

With the village gathered around, the chief greeted William and his companions. They were ushered into the chief's tepee, where the trading would take place. The men sat in a circle around the fire, with William Bent in the place of honor to the chief's left.

The young traveler Lewis Garrard, who was just two years older than Susan Magoffin, had accompanied William Bent to this chief's lodge during the year before Susan's stay at Bent's Fort. In his journal Garrard described the welcome he received:

> Water was handed us to drink, as they suppose a traveler must be thirsty after riding; then meat was set before us, as they think a tired man needs refreshment. When we had finished, the pipe was passed around, during which soothing pastime the news were asked.

William Bent offered gifts of coffee and sugar, two items that the Cheyenne could not obtain otherwise. Then Cheyenne women entered with armloads of buffalo robes they had prepared. Prices were set by counting sticks to determine how many robes would be traded for the mirrors, knives, or beads brought by the trader.

Next the Cheyenne men bargained for personal items, including glass beads for making necklaces and bracelets. They bargained for blankets, especially Navajo blankets that the Bent, St. Vrain, and Company traders had obtained at Santa Fe from tribes in the distant deserts of New Mexico and Arizona. Sometimes they bargained for small wooden barrels of whiskey and for hunting rifles.

Over the years the Cheyennes and the other Plains tribes experienced changes in their lifestyles. Not all of the changes were for the better. The more buffalo the Cheyennes killed for robes, the more white traders came to do business with them and the more dependent the Cheyennes became upon the traders. By the end of the 1800s the profitable trading would backfire on the Plains tribes, and their nomadic lives would be ended. Many

Cheyennes would be reminded of an ancient legend. A Cheyenne wise man had once predicted a meeting with people whose skin was white and whose customs were different from their own. According to the legend, great harm would come to the Cheyenne people because of this meeting.

In August of 1846, the summer of Susan Magoffin's visit, William Bent's Cheyenne friend Yellow Wolf also made a sad prediction. At the fort he spoke to Bent and a group of soldiers from the Army of the West. Yellow Wolf warned that the buffalo were becoming angry with his people. The Cheyenne hunters were killing so many buffalo for robes, he said, that his people could no longer consume all the meat as food. They were taking the robes and leaving the buffalo carcasses to rot. Because of this, Yellow Wolf predicted, the buffalo would soon leave the Plains, and the Cheyennes would starve. Indeed, in 1840 one trader in St. Louis had obtained robes from 67,000 buffalo. Yellow Wolf's concern for his people moved him to work closely with the white traders to find a solution. He was so concerned about overhunting the buffalo that he even offered to pay an interpreter at Bent's Fort to teach his people to farm the prairie and raise cattle as whites did. Yellow Wolf's offer may have been laughed at by William Bent and his soldier guests or merely ignored. Since the hunting continued, it is fair to say that Yellow Wolf's warning about the buffalo was certainly ignored by his own people.

5 The Army of the West on the Santa Fe Trail

The year 1846 was one of tremendous political changes for the lands and peoples of the Southwest. Then again, the Southwest had already gone through many such changes. In the early 1500s Mexico was conquered by the armies of Spain, the conquistadors. In 1821, Mexico won its independence from Spain. In turn, Texas, a province of Mexico, fought for and won its independence from Mexico in 1836. However, Mexico never acknowledged that independence, continuing to claim Texas as its own.

Most Texans wanted their territory to become part of the United States—that is, to be annexed. This annexation was officially completed in the eventful year of 1846. Because of it, the Mexican government declared war on the United States. That is what led U.S. President James K. Polk to ask Congress for a declaration of war against Mexico in May of that year. Even before President Polk's request was honored by Congress, the Army of the West was moving down the Santa Fe Trail.

A recently promoted general, Stephen Watts Kearny, had organized the men and materials needed to support an invasion of Mexico. The governor of Missouri had also put out a call for volunteers to fill the ranks, and more than eight hundred men answered. They enlisted for a period of one year and called themselves the Missouri Mounted Volunteers.

Each volunteer provided his own horse and his own supplies. Although promised uniforms, the men never received them. It was said the volunteers "started out in buckskins and ended up in tatters." Each volunteer took special care of his horse. If a horse died, it was difficult if not impossible to replace. Horses were sold in Missouri for about $40. At Bent's Fort a similar animal might cost $100 or even more. Even "very ordinary mules" brought $70 or $80 there. Since army pay was less than $16 a month, a volunteer could not afford to buy another mount along the trail. If he could not replace his horse, he would have to be reassigned to the infantry.

Men in the infantry marched wherever they went. They had to walk hundreds of miles from St. Louis down the Santa Fe Trail to Bent's Fort before even getting to the Mexican border.

Although loosely attached to the Army of the West, the Missouri Mounted Volunteers elected their own officers. Their leader was Colonel Alexander Doniphan. Doniphan's troops were noted for their lack of military "spit and polish," but before the war was over, newspaper accounts of their fighting spirit would make them national heroes.

By July 1846 the Army of the West was rumbling down the Santa Fe Trail with more than one hundred wagons and eight hundred beef cattle. Kearny led this massive parade toward Bent's Fort, which made a perfect supply depot. From there he planned to cross the Arkansas River and lead an invasion of Mexico.

At the outbreak of the Mexican War, Stephen Watts Kearny was made commander of the Army of the West, with the rank of brigadier general.

Eighteen-year-old Marcellus Ball Edwards was a private in the Missouri Volunteers. He kept a journal of his experiences with the Army of the West. He noted that the size of the army caused problems along the trail. "We have . . . experienced great inconveniences," he wrote, "from want of wood and water, and our horses for want of grass." Once the army reached the Arkansas River there was plenty of good water. Firewood, however, was still a problem. "There is but little timber on this stream," Marcellus wrote. "We have been compelled to camp without it several times." The shortage of firewood forced the men to burn "dry excrement of buffalo." Marcellus noted that the buffalo chip "answer[s] a very good purpose: but it has no flame, it would not serve well to warm in cold weather. But it seems to impart a peculiar, pleasant flavor to meat broiled on its smothering heat."

Marcellus Ball Edwards was camped near Bent's Fort when Susan and Samuel Magoffin arrived there. It is possible that the Magoffins passed the spot where Marcellus was camped. Susan wrote on July 27:

> . . . we passed the soldiers['] encampment, another novel sight to me, perhaps there were fifty or more little tents stretched with here and there a wagon, and a little shade made of tree limbs. The idle soldiers stretched under these, others were out watering horses staked about the camp, some were drying clothes in the sun. . . .

Even soldiers who were in the regular army received few benefits. Like those observed by Susan Magoffin, most soldiers cared for their own animals, did their own laundry, and prepared their own meals. The army provided food that could be stored for long periods and did not need to be kept cold. A soldier's diet consisted of beans, salt pork, coffee, and hardtack (a baked mixture of flour, water, and salt). Sometimes, at places like Bent's Fort, soldiers could trade for eggs or fresh meat.

This cut was made for Doniphan's Expedition, *a book published in 1850. The caption indicated it was "a sample of Colonel Doniphan's command."*

If the soldiers' diet seems poor, it was. In fact, their diet was a bigger threat to their well-being than enemy bullets. Because soldiers ate almost no fresh fruits or vegetables, they often suffered from scurvy. Diseases like dysentery, typhoid, and cholera, all carried by polluted drinking water, were also common along the trail. These diseases struck suddenly, and a person who appeared healthy in the morning could be dead by mid-afternoon. Susan Magoffin reflected on this while recovering from the loss of her baby, when she wrote, "One must have great faith in their Creator . . . not to feel sad and uneasy to see such things passing around them,—their fellow creatures snatched off in a moment without warning almost." The soldiers who recovered quickly were sent ahead to rejoin their regiments. Those who recovered more slowly were sent back over the same miles of trail they had already covered.

For some who became ill, recovery would not come at all. "During our stay here [at Bent's Fort]," wrote Marcellus Ball Edwards, "one death occurred." He described the funeral of his fellow soldier as follows:

> The day after [he died] he was buried with the honors of war. . . . Upon the shoulders of four men was borne the body of the deceased, the national flag serving as his pall, a blanket his coffin and winding sheet. His horse, saddled with the arms on the saddle and his boots inverted in the stirrup, was led by two men. This led off, followed by the five companies. Three volleys were fired over the grave, and the procession returned.

Breaking military rules called for severe punishments. Marcellus described what happened to a group of soldiers who traded for liquor at the fort, even though the liquor cost $24 a gallon (about $6 a liter). They got drunk and started to fight. When officers tried to arrest them, they "shared equally the blows that were passing." The men described by Marcellus were tried before

Although the Santa Fe Trail ended in the benign climate of New Mexico, it began in Independence, Missouri. At certain times of year weather could make travel even more treacherous than it already was, as evidenced by this supply wagon train attempting to cross the Great Plains in a snowstorm.

a military court and convicted. They were sentenced to walk guard duty from morning to night. As they marched they had to carry saddlebags filled with 40 pounds (18 kilograms) of sand on their backs. This punishment continued for five days.

The Army of the West left Bent's Fort on July 31 and crossed the Arkansas River into territory claimed by Mexico. According to Susan Magoffin, "They made rather a grand show." In her diary Susan described their noisy departure:

"The trumpet sounded oft and loud," she wrote, and "swords rattled in their sheaths."

6 The Mexican Trade

A few days after the Army of the West left Bent's Fort, Samuel Magoffin ordered his wagons and carts to continue their trip down the Santa Fe Trail. Susan was healthy enough to travel again, and the army would provide protection for the travelers. Six miles from the fort the trail took the caravan across the shallow Arkansas River and into territory claimed by Mexico but now in dispute.

At their first camp south of the border Susan wrote in her diary, "I am now entirely out of 'The States,' into a new country. The crossing of the Arkansas was an event in my life, I have never met with before; the separating me from my own dear native land."

As the Magoffins followed the trail south and west, the land became more and more like a desert. The green grass of the prairie was replaced by cactus and sand hills. Intense heat on the desert sand formed mirages that fooled the eye, making the weary travelers see imaginary ponds of cool water on the horizon. Even

Susan's dog, Ring, must have noticed the different surroundings. During the second night away from Bent's Fort, Ring kept the Magoffins awake with "awful and unearthly yells and howlings."

Before reaching its destination, the Santa Fe Trail rose through a wooded mountain pass called the Raton. The trail became steep and rocky, and the progress of the wagons slowed to half a mile an hour. This gave Susan the chance to leave the caravan and ride horseback alone through the pine woods. Ring "kept strict watch for Indians, bear, panther, wolves, &c.," Susan wrote, "and would not even leave my side as if conscious I had no other protector at hand."

On August 18, 1846, General Stephen Watts Kearny and the Army of the West marched into Santa Fe, capturing it without a fight. On August 30 the Magoffin caravan entered the town. It was not yet clear how war with Mexico would affect the bustling trade; but because the American Army had taken over Santa Fe, the Magoffins had no trouble entering the town or finding safe lodgings.

Santa Fe is one of the oldest towns in North America. The Spanish had explored the area as early as the 1530s. They were the first to bring horses to the continent. The offspring of those first horses eventually spread north through the Plains, where tribes like the Cheyenne acquired them. The Spanish also brought cattle with them. When cattle wandered away and became lost, their Spanish and Mexican owners naturally had to ride off to look for them. A Spanish or Mexican man who hunted the dry grasslands for lost cows was called a *vaquero* (vah-KAYR-oh). Today we also know him by his English name: cowboy.

The town of Santa Fe was founded in 1609 or 1610. The Palace of the Governors, built in 1610, is one of the oldest Spanish buildings still standing in North America. When the Spanish government built the palace, it borrowed techniques used in building

This 1845 engraving depicts the arrival of a wagon caravan in Santa Fe. The wagons are laden with goods that will be exchanged for mules, furs, gold, and silver. Note the travelers' elation as the end of their 780-mile (1,260-kilometer) journey is in sight.

the local Zuni homes called pueblos. Like the pueblos, the palace had thick adobe walls and projecting wooden beams supporting a flat roof. But the palace also had a portal, or covered sidewalk, similar to those of medieval monasteries in Spain. It was this thick-walled adobe style that William Bent later imitated in the construction of Bent's Fort.

Under Spanish rule Santa Fe and the neighboring village of San Fernandez flourished as trading centers. San Fernandez, later known as Taos, hosted trading fairs each summer. Traders from

Chihuahua, hundreds of miles to the south, arrived in two-wheeled carts called *carretas* filled with dainty slippers, shawls, *mantillas* (lace scarves), and El Paso wine. French trappers came down from the mountains to the north. Their pack mules carried pelts, beads, knives, and illegal guns to trade. The local residents offered precious turquoise stones and bits of silver. Navajos from the deserts to the west brought their handmade blankets and pottery. From the plains east of Santa Fe and Taos, Comanches brought buffalo robes. The mountain Utes sold captives from other tribes as slaves.

Under Spanish rule, however, Americans were not allowed into Mexico to trade. Then, in 1821, when the Mexicans won independence from Spain, the Santa Fe Trail was opened. Traders from Missouri arrived in growing numbers despite the high tax they were charged to do business. Mexican traders at that time also began to use the trail, seeking out Native American villages on the Plains where they offered dried pumpkin and corn in exchange for buffalo robes and dried meat. Sometimes the Mexican traders offered brightly colored feathers from exotic tropical birds. On other trips the Mexican traders might offer seashells, which were used in making earrings.

By the 1830s Santa Fe traders were also making trips east along the trail all the way to Missouri. The Santa Fe traders loaded their goods on packsaddles carried by entire "trains" of mules. Because the mules were easily frightened by sudden movements or strange sights, they often had to be blindfolded to keep them calm on the trail.

By 1846 the western end of the Santa Fe Trail was bustling. Santa Fe and Taos continued to attract the Native American, Spanish, and Mexican peoples, but now included in that mixture—because of the trail—were English-speaking Americans like Samuel and Susan Magoffin.

Some Americans ridiculed the dusty, rowdy town at the end of the trail. Aside from business, there seemed to be few activities in Santa Fe other than gambling and drinking alcohol. It was nothing more, some said, than a "prairie-dog town."

Susan Magoffin found the people of Santa Fe friendly and helpful, though she noticed many differences between life in Santa Fe and life back in "the States." For example, the houses contained little furniture, since tables, chairs, beds, and the like were difficult to transport from the distant manufacturing cities. Walls inside the houses were draped with calico cloth to keep the gypsum whitewash from rubbing onto people's clothes.

At dinner parties Susan attended in this remote town, guests would wear fine clothing and jewelry, and the knives and forks they ate with were often solid silver. Men and women dined separately, which Susan felt was proper. But she was shocked that the women, as well as the men, smoked small cigars called *cigarillos,* something that women simply did not do in the United States at that time. Meals consisted of foods that are still familiar: tortillas, chili, and *frijoles* (beans), with fiery red peppers to add spice. A common drink was *atole,* made by stirring cornmeal into boiling milk or water. It was such a favorite that traders called it *el café de los Mexicanos* ("the coffee of the Mexicans").

Both Santa Fe and Taos were famous for their *fandangos.* A *fandango* was a party at which everyone danced the night away. Music was provided by local musicians, who formed an "orchestra" of guitars and fiddles. The same musicians might also play for weddings and funerals.

One American trader who enjoyed life at the western end of the Santa Fe Trail was Charles Bent. In 1835 he had settled down permanently in Taos. He had married a Mexican woman named Mariá Ignacia Jaramillo, who was a widow with one daughter. They moved into a house north of the plaza in the center of town.

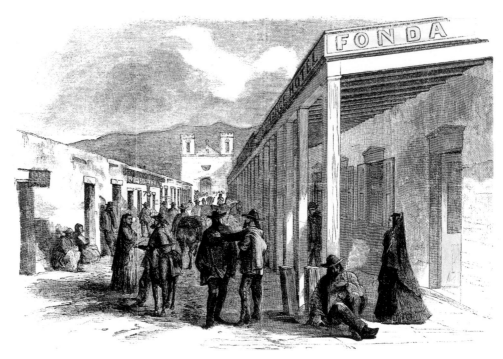

An 1860s woodcut showing the literal end of the Santa Fe trail at the La Fonda Hotel. St. Francis Cathedral is at the end of the street.

Together Charles Bent and Mariá Ignacia had five children, although two of them died in infancy.

Charles Bent, like Samuel Magoffin, made his living from trading. In Taos it was Charles Bent who handled business affairs for Bent, St. Vrain, and Company. He checked the incoming boxes and barrels of cotton cloth, knives, and household goods shipped from the United States. He then did his best to make a profit for the company by trading those items for wool, handicraft items, and mules that could be traded or sold at Bent's Fort or back in Missouri. The Mexican trade was often dangerous and always hard work. For the few years it lasted, it was also highly profitable for businessmen like the Bents and Samuel Magoffin.

7 Bent's Fort in Ruins

Bent's Fort was practically taken over by the United States Army during the war with Mexico. It was used as an important part of the supply line supporting U.S. troops in and around Santa Fe. In the two-week period after General Kearny's troops captured Santa Fe in August 1846, no fewer than fifty wagons full of supplies rolled past Bent's Fort on the Santa Fe Trail. Normal business at the fort was totally disrupted.

Colonel Alexander Doniphan and his Missouri Mounted Volunteers were ordered farther south into Mexico in December. The Volunteers marched 2,000 miles (about 3,200 kilometers) and fought two major battles before reaching the Gulf of Mexico. By the end of 1847, the one-year enlistments of Doniphan's volunteers had ended. None of them reenlisted. Like his comrades, journal writer Marcellus Ball Edwards returned home.

General Kearny continued to California to complete the American conquest of the Southwest. The war with Mexico lasted two years ending in February 1848, when the Treaty of Guadalupe Hidalgo was signed. The United States was victorious and took a huge tract of land from Mexico. The area includes most of the present states of New Mexico, Arizona, California, Utah, and Nevada, and parts of Colorado and Wyoming. Mexico also recognized Texas as part of the United States.

Susan and Samuel Magoffin continued their 1846 journey by traveling south from Santa Fe on the Chihuahua Trail. They spent time in the small Mexican town of Matamoras, across the Rio Grande River from present-day Brownsville, Texas. On September 8, 1847, Susan wrote in her diary for the last time. She became ill shortly afterward.

Susan was again expecting a baby. During her illness she gave birth to a son, but he soon died. When Susan recovered, she and Samuel traveled by ship to New Orleans and returned home to Missouri. The long trip down the Santa Fe Trail and through Mexico had harmed Susan's health. In 1851 she gave birth to Jane, a healthy daughter. However, she never recovered from the birth of a fourth child, a daughter named Susan after her mother. In 1855, nine years after becoming the first white woman to travel the Santa Fe Trail, Susan Shelby Magoffin died. She was only twenty-eight years old. Susan Magoffin's diary was kept by one of her daughters until 1926, when her personal view of history was published for all to read.

Yellow Wolf, the Cheyenne warrior who had first suggested a location for William Bent's trading fort, lived to be more than eighty years old. In 1864 he was killed by soldiers of the First Colorado Volunteers in a massacre of peaceful Indians encamped at Sand Creek, in eastern Colorado. His prediction and warning about the dangers of overhunting the buffalo sadly came true for both his own people and the white traders.

It is estimated that in 1850 about twenty million buffalo roamed the prairies of North America. By 1889, well within one human lifetime, government authorities could find only 551 living buffalo. Demand for buffalo robes and, later, the deadly accuracy of "professional" white hunters had all but killed off this proud beast.

Charles Bent was appointed the first American governor of New Mexico by General Stephen Watts Kearny on September 22, 1846. He most likely received this appointment for his support of what was called Manifest Destiny—the idea that the United States should expand America's expansion westward to the Pacific Ocean. He served as governor for only four months before being killed in an uprising at Taos in January 1847.

Bent, St. Vrain, and Company was never paid for any of the goods or services it provided to the U.S. Army. During the war, Ceran St. Vrain offered to sell Bent's Fort to the U.S. government for $15,000. Although the government refused the offer, William Bent never forgave St. Vrain for not consulting with him about the sale. In late 1848 or early 1849, St. Vrain turned his part of the business over to William Bent.

The discovery of gold at Sutter's Mill in California in 1848 also affected life at Bent's Fort. The next year floods of gold seekers and settlers began pouring over the Oregon and Santa Fe trails bound for the Pacific Coast. The same year a deadly cholera epidemic broke out in St. Louis. As people moved west along the trails, the disease traveled with them. William Bent, who may have been heading toward St. Louis, cut short a trading trip and returned to his fort to avoid the plague. Yellow Woman, whom William had married after the death of his first wife, and his three youngest children were already there. She had just returned from a tribal gathering and was panic-stricken. Yellow Woman had seen men, women, and children at the gathering suddenly double over in pain and die in agony of the "big cramps"—cholera. Within weeks of the outbreak in St. Louis, cholera spread across the plains. It killed half of the Southern Cheyennes.

William Bent's "Indian trade" was forever damaged. He realized that the fort could no longer support itself. In August 1849, William loaded his goods into as many as twenty wagons and prepared to abandon the "adobe castle." There is a mystery about what happened next. Some historians say that before he left the fort, William burned barrels of tar, believing that smoke from such fires would rid the air of cholera. The fires from the tar barrels may have spread and burned the fort to the ground.

Others say William ignited kegs of powder he had placed along the walls of the fortress. In either case, on August 21, 1849, Bent's Fort was destroyed in a burst of flames.

William Bent eventually built a new fort for trading, although it never gained the fame of the original. In 1859 he was made an Indian agent for the U.S. government. Unlike most agents, who cared little for the Native Americans they were hired to help, William Bent sincerely tried to defend the people whose world had been all but crushed by the advance of white settlement.

In the 1860s William Bent also took up ranching in the area of the old fort. Just before his sixtieth birthday, in 1869, he was leading a caravan of wagons back from New Mexico. His route included the difficult Raton, the mountain pass traveled by Susan Magoffin many years earlier. Although he completed the trip and returned home to his ranch near the Purgatory River, he came down with pneumonia. On May 19, 1869, William Bent died, a wealthy and respected man who had lived—and helped to make—the history of the American West.

8 Afterword: Bent's Fort Reconstructed

The adobe ruins of Bent's Old Fort gradually melted away. By the early 1900s all that remained were small mounds of earth vaguely indicating where walls had once been. In 1912 the La Junta (Colorado) Chapter of the Daughters of the American Revolution set up a marker at the site. A rancher donated the land the fort was on to the D.A.R. in the 1920s.

Many people dreamed of rebuilding Bent's Old Fort. In 1954 the fort site was bought by the Colorado State Historical Society, from the La Junta D.A.R. for one dollar. They began a series of archaeological excavations with the help of local colleges. Many artifacts were uncovered, and the general outline of the fort was exposed for the first time in a hundred years. Some thought was given simply to preserve the ruins as an archaeological site. The society gradually acquired additional land around the fort. Due to lack of money, little more was done.

The photograph above shows the front entrance of Bent's Old Fort as it appears today. Below is the reconstructed central plaza where much of the business of the fort was once conducted. Notice the fur press in the middle of the plaza.

In the late 1950s the National Park Service was approached about taking over the Bent's Fort site. In June 1960, President Dwight D. Eisenhower signed a bill naming Bent's Old Fort a national historic site. During the 1960s additional archaeological work was conducted. More than 35,000 artifacts were collected. Attempts were made to keep the freshly exposed, original adobe walls from eroding. None were completely successful. Funds were lacking for additional preservation or reconstruction.

All this changed as 1976 approached. That year was to be special for both Colorado and the nation. Colorado celebrated 100 years of statehood (centennial) while the nation celebrated 200 years of independence (bicentennial). It was decided that a reconstruction of Bent's Fort would be an appropriate way to mark both events. The reconstruction project was finally funded, and the first adobe brick of the reconstruction of Bent's Fort was laid on July 5, 1975.

Since the reconstruction of Bent's Fort on the original site would destroy any remaining artifacts, care was taken to collect and preserve as many as possible. Small pieces of the original wall were incorporated into the reconstruction.

Tremendous care was taken to produce as accurate a reconstruction of the fort as possible. Since there were no photographs of the original fort, researchers had to depend on firsthand accounts of those who had visited the fort, such as Susan Magoffin. A few rough sketches had been made by visitors to the fort. George Bent, one of William Bent's sons, produced one of the most famous sketches of the fort in 1908. It was done from memory since the fort was destroyed in 1849, when George was only six years old.

Lieutenant James W. Abert was twenty-six years old when he came to Bent's Fort with General Stephen Watts Kearny. He caught "the fever" and spent August 1846 at the fort. While he was recovering, Abert made sketches of life at the fort. He also recorded the dimensions of the structure. Abert's observations were very important in planning the reconstruction.

Bent's Old Fort

Bent's Old Fort has been reconstructed as accurately as possible to look as it did in 1845–1846, when Bent, St. Vrain, and Company was at the zenith of its power, both commercially and politically.

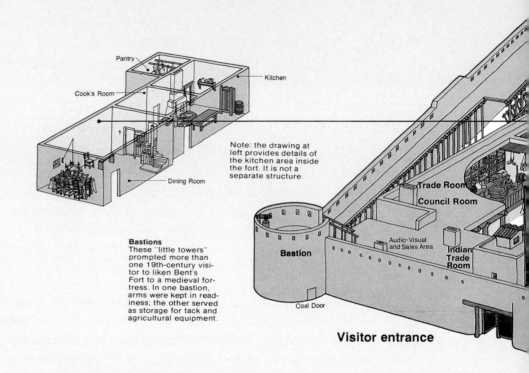

Cook's Room
Black Charlotte, the fort cook, and her husband, Dick Green, lived in the room just off the kitchen. The Greens had been Bent family slaves in Missouri. Charlotte was famous from Longs Peak to the Spanish Peaks for her slapjacks and pumpkin pie.

Dining Room
This room, the largest in the fort, was used by traders, trappers, hunters, and all employees. Usually simple fare was provided; but on occasion elaborate meals were served here for celebrated visitors such as John C. Fremont on July 4, 1844, and Francis Parkman who, in 1846, was delighted to find "a table laid with a white cloth." One traveler used "Knives and forks and plates" here for the first time in 50 days.

Kitchen
Dried buffalo meat and bread made of coarse flour were prepared here and considered standard fare at the fort. Opinions about the bread differed, but the Comanche Chief Old Wolf definitely considered it fit only "to fuel a smoke-fire for coloring buckskins."

Note: the drawing at left provides details of the kitchen area inside the fort. It is not a separate structure.

Bastions
These "little towers" prompted more than one 19th-century visitor to liken Bent's Fort to a medieval fortress. In one bastion, arms were kept in readiness; the other served as storage for tack and agricultural equipment.

Trade Room and Council Room

"In the store of the Fort—presumably for sale to trappers and travelers, and for use of the proprietors," William Bent's son, George, remembered, are "such unusual luxuries as butter crackers, Bent's water crackers, candies of various sorts, and most remarkable of all, great jars of preserved ginger...." The chief items of trade were buffalo robes, beaver pelts, and horses that the Indians, Mexicans, and mountain men traded for factory-made goods from St. Louis.

The council room, located next to the trade room, served as a meeting place where terms and prices were set between the trader and representatives of the Indian tribes. Peace talks were occasionally held here, and Susan Magoffin mentioned its use as temporary sleeping quarters for a large number of men.

William Bent's Quarters

There are actually two rooms here: William Bent's office, with an Eastern-style fireplace, and his adjoining bedroom. One traveler reported that the owners of the fort "laid on pallets of straw" and Spanish blankets. This was a Spanish colonial custom, as was the calico wainscoting used to keep the wash on adobe walls from rubbing off on the occupant's clothing.

Blacksmith and Carpenter Shops

As the principal outpost of American civilization on the southwestern frontier, Bent's Old Fort offered all kinds of accommodations to travelers. By 1846 the fort was a fairly self-sufficient institution. Employing about 60 to 100 persons, it required the services of numerous tradesmen such as wheelwrights, carpenters, coopers, blacksmiths, and gunsmiths. Lt. James Abert, who stayed at the fort for several weeks in the summer of 1846, said "The ring of the blacksmith's hammer and the noise from the wagoner's shop were incessant." A blacksmith, carpenter, and related tradesmen worked in these areas throughout the fort's existence; a gunsmith operated here only briefly, during the later years.

Laborers' Quarters

Laborers from Santa Fe and Taos built and maintained the fort. Their wives assisted in the day-to-day operation, did cleaning and cooking.

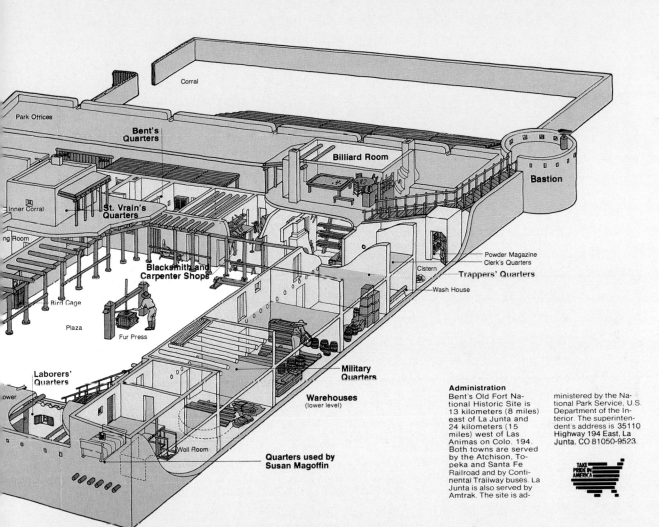

Corral

Park Offices

Bent's Quarters

Billiard Room

Bastion

Inner Corral

St. Vrain's Quarters

Powder Magazine
Clerk's Quarters
Trappers' Quarters

ng Room

Cistern

Blacksmith and Carpenter Shops

Wash House

Bird Cage

Plaza

Fur Press

Military Quarters

Laborers' Quarters

Warehouses
(lower level)

ower

Woll Room

Quarters used by Susan Magoffin

Administration
Bent's Old Fort National Historic Site is 13 kilometers (8 miles) east of La Junta and 24 kilometers (15 miles) west of Las Animas on Colo. 194. Both towns are served by the Atchison, Topeka and Santa Fe Railroad and by Continental Trailway buses. La Junta is also served by Amtrak. The site is administered by the National Park Service, U.S. Department of the Interior. The superintendent's address is 35110 Highway 194 East, La Junta, CO 81050-9523.

TAKE PRIDE IN AMERICA

Trappers' Quarters
Many of the mountain men who depended on the fort for supplies were "freetrappers"—independent souls who paused here just long enough to sell their furs and sample the "civilized" life before they were off again for the mountains with another year's supplies.

Military Quarters
When Kearney's Army of the West reached Bent's Fort in the summer of 1846, it brought with it evidence of the rigors of the trail. Twenty-one men were sick with dysentery and scurvy alone. Six would die here. When the army moved on, those unable to travel were left behind to convalesce.

Quarters used by Susan Magoffin
Mrs. Magoffin's room—like the adjoining four on this floor and several on the first—usually served as temporary quarters for travelers and fort employees. Most of these rooms were small and sparsely furnished, if at all.

Susan Magoffin, enroute to Santa Fe with her husband, spent her 19th birthday here in 1846. She lost a baby during her 10-day stay, but still managed to keep a meticulous diary that stands as one of the most complete descriptions we have of the 1846 fort. Her own furnishings—a bed, chairs, a wash basin, and table— were moved into the room for her convalescence, and she took all of her meals there. The room had a dirt floor and featured two windows, an unusual distinction.

Billiard Room
Ranking second in pleasure only to drink and tobacco was gambling, and the billiard room was, at once, the most unusual and the most popular feature at Bent's Fort. "The love of gaming seems inherent in our very natures," the young Lewis Garrard remarked. The original billiard table (the one in the room now is a reproduction) was brought to the fort from St. Louis in the 1830s.

Warehouses
This row of rooms was used for the storage of furs and trade goods during the winters. In the spring these storehouses were gradually emptied as trading expeditions departed to the surrounding Indian tribes, and wagon trains loaded with furs set out across the plains for St. Louis. For a brief period in the 1840s this area was also used for storage of military supplies.

Once actual reconstruction was begun, great care was taken to be sure everything was as authentic to 1846 as possible. Even the adobe used to make the bricks was carefully reproduced. Cottonwood and pine logs were gathered for use as beams. Antique tools from the 1840s were used so that the marks they left on the beams would be true to the period. Original plaster colors for inside walls were reproduced, using information gathered during the archaeological work. Hardware, such as hinges and latches, were reproduced by skilled blacksmiths.

Not only did the fort have to be rebuilt, but it also had to be furnished. Again many sources were consulted to be sure that everything that was placed in the fort was authentic. Drawings and first-hand accounts were again consulted. Some items, like the large billiard table, were well documented. Ordinary items in daily use were not considered important enough to mention in the letters and diaries of the time. Artifacts from the excavations at Bent's Fort, as well as the study of other buildings from the period, gave additional clues as to the kinds of everyday things people used in 1846.

Very few actual antiques are on display at Bent's Fort. Susan Magoffin's room is an exception. Exact reproductions were used throughout the fort. This is partially due to the number of items needed for display. The recommended number of trade goods alone was more than 30,000 items. Each item on display is an exact duplicate of the antique it represents.

On July 25, 1976, the state of Colorado and the National Park Service dedicated the reconstructed Old Bent's Fort. As a result of the work of many people and organizations, visitors to Old Bent's Fort today experience what life was like in 1846. The fort often plays host to "pioneers" dressed in period costume who "live" 1846.

You can visit Bent's Old Fort today. It is located 7 miles (11 kilometers) east of La Junta, Colorado, off U.S. Highway 50.

Bibliography

Barber, Barton H., ed. *Reluctant Frontiersman, James Ross Larkin on the Santa Fe Trail 1856–57.* Albuquerque: University of New Mexico Press, 1990.

Benson, Maxine, Duane A. Smith, and Carl Ubbelohde. *A Colorado History.* Boulder: Pruett Publishing Company, 1972.

Bent's Old Fort. The State Historical Society of Colorado, 1979.

Berthrong, Donald J. *The Southern Cheyenne.* Norman: University of Oklahoma Press, 1963.

Bieber, Ralph P., ed. *Marching with the Army of the West, 1846–1848.* Glendale: The Arthur H. Clark Co., 1936.

Blevins, Winfred. *Dictionary of the American West.* New York: Facts on File, 1993.

Brown, Robert L. *Jeep Trails to Colorado Ghost Towns.* Caldwell, Idaho: The Caxton Printers, Ltd., 1968.

DeVoto, Bernard. *The Year of Decision: 1846.* Boston: Little, Brown and Company, 1943.

Drumm, Stella M., ed. *Down the Santa Fe Trail and Into Mexico: The Diary of Susan Shelby Magoffin, 1846–1847.* Lincoln: University of Nebraska Press, 1962.

Fulton, Maurice Garland. *Diaries and Letters of Josiah Gregg.* Norman: University of Oklahoma Press, 1941.

Garrard, Lewis H. *Wah-To-Yah and the Taos Trail.* Norman: University of Oklahoma Press, 1955.

Gregg, Josiah. *Commerce of the Prairies.* Norman: University of Oklahoma Press, 1954.

Grinnell, George Bird. *The Cheyenne Indians: Their History and Ways of Life.* 2 vols. New Haven: Yale University Press, 1923.

————. *The Fighting Cheyennes.* New York: Charles Scribner's Sons, 1915.

Horgan, Paul. *The Centuries of Santa Fe.* New York: E.P. Dutton and Company, 1956.

Lavender, David S. *Bent's Fort.* Lincoln: University of Nebraska Press, 1954.

McHugh, Tom. *The Time of the Buffalo.* New York: Alfred A. Knopf, Inc., 1972.

Nevin, David. *The Mexican War.* Alexandria, Va.: Time-Life Books, 1978.

————. *The Soldiers.* New York: Time-Life Books, 1973.

Sandoz, Mari. *Cheyenne Autumn.* New York: McGraw-Hill Book Company, Inc., 1953.

The Spanish West. New York: Time-Life Books, 1976.

Weber, David J. *The Mexican Frontier, 1821–1846: The American Southwest Under Mexico.* Albuquerque: University of New Mexico Press, 1982.

Wetzel, David N., ed. *The Santa Fe Trail: New Perspectives.* Denver: Colorado Historical Society, 1987.

Index

Buffalo, 18, 20, 24, 38, *39*, 42, 43, 58-59

Catholic Church, 27
Cheyenne Indians, 15, 20, 23-24, 27, 36-38, 40, 42-43, 60
Chihuahua, 54
Chihuahua Trail, 58
Cholera, 59-60
Chouteau, Pierre, 27
Colorado State Historical Society, 61
Comanche Indians, 24, *34*, 54
Cowboys, 52
Cree Indians, 37

Daughters of the American Revolution, 61
Diseases, 49, 59-60
Dodd, Old Belzy, 34
Doniphan, Alexander, 45, 57
Doniphan's Expedition, 48

Edwards, Marcellus Ball, 47, 49, 57
Eisenhower, Dwight D., 63

Fandangos, 55
First Colorado Volunteers, 58
French and Indian War, 17
Fur trade, 17-20

Gambling, 33, 34
Garrard, Lewis, 35, 42
Gold, 59
Green, Andrew, 28-29
Green, Charlotte, 29, 31, 32, 35
Green, Dick, 28-29
Guadalupe Hidalgo, Treaty of (1848), 58

Hairy Rope Clan, 23
Horses, 37-38

Independence, Missouri, 9, 26

Jaramillo, Mariá Ignacia, 55-56

Kearny, Stephen Watts, 45, *46,* 52, 57, 59
Kiowa Indians, 23, 24, 37

Laidlaw, William, 27
La Junta (Colorado) Chapter of the Daughters of the American Revolution, 61
Lisa, Manuel, 17
Little Raven, *29*

Magoffin, Jane, 58
Magoffin, Samuel, 9, 10, 12, 14, 30, 51, 58
Magoffin, Susan, 58
Magoffin, Susan Shelby, 9-10, *11,* 12-16, 26, 30-33, 35, 36, 47, 49-52, 55, 58, 63
Manifest Destiny, 59
Matamoras, 58
Mexican trade, 51-56
Mexico, 9, 12, 28, 44, 45, 51, 57-58
Mississippi River, 17
Missouri Fur Company, 17
Missouri Mounted Volunteers, 45, 47, 57
Missouri River, 17
Mis-stan-stur, 40, *41*
Mormon Church, 26
Mountain men, 15, 18, 20

National Park Service, 61, 66
Native Americans (*see* specific tribes)
Navajo Indians, 42, 54

Pawnee Indians, 27, 37
Plains Indians, 31
Polk, James K., 44
Prairie Apache Indians, 24
Pueblo, Colorado, 20